Living on Farms

By Allan Fowler

Consultant
Linda Cornwell, Coordinator of School Quality
and Professional Improvement
Indiana State Teachers Association

ᏘP Children's Press®
A Division of Grolier Publishing
New York   London   Hong Kong   Sydney
Danbury, Connecticut

Visit Children's Press® on the Internet at:
http://publishing.grolier.com

Designer: Herman Adler Design Group

Library of Congress Cataloging-in-Publication Data

Fowler, Allan.
    Living on farms / by Allan Fowler.
      p. cm.   — (Rookie read-about geography)
    Summary: A simple introduction to the history, animals, machines,
products, and importance of farms.
    ISBN 0-516-21564-7 (lib. bdg.)   0-516-27085-0 (pbk.)
    1. Farms Juvenile literature. 2. Agriculture Juvenile literature.
[1. Farms. 2. Farm life. 3. Agriculture.] I. Title. II. Series.
S519.F68   2000
630–dc21   99-38878
                                              CIP

GROLIER
PUBLISHING

This is what many farms
used to look like. A single
family owned the farm and
lived on it and worked on it.

As soon as the farmer's children were old enough, they would help with the chores.

They might milk the cows, feed the animals, plant the seeds, or pull the weeds.

There was always work to be done.

Many different vegetables and fruits would grow on a family farm.

There would be livestock like cattle, pigs, and sheep.

And poultry like chickens, ducks, and turkeys. The family's food came from their own farm.

Sheep

Turkeys

8

Some farms are still like that. But today we get most of our food from much larger farms.

Many of these big farms grow just one type of food.

There are wheat farms, corn farms, and potato farms. There are farms for every kind of vegetable or fruit.

A wheat farm

Cows hooked up to milking machines

The milk you drink comes from dairy farms. There machines milk the cows.

Herds of beef cattle graze on big ranches.

We get eggs, chickens, ducks, and turkeys from poultry farms. There are even fish farms!

Feed for farm animals
is stored in tall, round
buildings called silos.

silo

This is how farmers used to plow.

A long time ago, more
people lived on farms
than in cities.

Horses or oxen pulled
the plows.

People had to do almost
all the other work by hand.

Now, fewer people have
to live on farms because
machines do so much of
the work.

Tractors pull plows that
break up the soil, and
planters drop in the seeds.

Big combines harvest,
or pick, wheat and other
grain crops.

Tractor planting seeds

Combines harvesting corn

Some farm jobs are still done by hand.

A lot of farmers pick fruit by hand so it doesn't get damaged.

Grapefruit tree

Farmers depend greatly on the weather.

Some crops, such as oranges and grapefruit, need warm weather.

They grow best in warm places like Florida and southern California.

Other crops, such as apples, potatoes, pumpkins, and corn, grow well where it's cooler.

Pumpkins

Irrigation ditch

All crops need water.
Where there isn't enough
rainfall, water must be
brought in from rivers
and lakes.

It flows through the
farm in pipes or ditches.

This is called irrigation.

Living on a farm means a lot of hard work. But eating the food you grow is a lot of fun . . . and it tastes great, too!

Words You Know

combines

dairy farm

irrigation ditch

sheep

30

silo

tractor

turkeys

wheat

Index

animals, 5
cattle, 6, 13
chickens, 6, 13
chores, 5
combines, 18
cows, 5, 12, 13
crops, 18, 23, 24, 27
dairy farms, 13
ducks, 6, 13
eggs, 13
farmer, 5, 20, 23
fish farms, 13
fruits, 6, 10, 20
grapefruit, 23
harvest, 18
horses, 17
irrigation, 27

livestock, 6
milk, 13
oranges, 23
oxen, 17
pigs, 6
plow, 17, 18
poultry, 6
poultry farms, 13
pumpkins, 24
ranches, 13
sheep, 6
silo, 14
tractors, 18, 19
turkeys, 6, 13
vegetables, 6, 10
wheat, 10, 18

About the Author

Allan Fowler is a freelance writer with a background in advertising. Born in New York, he now lives in Chicago and enjoys traveling.

Photo Credits